GOOD HUSBAND

GUIDE

13-Digit ISBN: 978-1-60433-205-6
10-Digit ISBN: 1-60433-205-0

This book may be ordered by mail
from the publisher.
Please include $2.50 for postage and handling.
Please support your local bookseller first!

Books published by
Cider Mill Press Book
Publishers are available at
special discounts for bulk
purchases in the United
States by corporations,
institutions, and other
organizations. For more
information, please contact
the publisher.

Cider Mill Press Book
Publishers
"Where good books
are ready for press"
12 Port Farm Road
Kennebunkport, Maine
04046

Visit us on the web!
www.cidermillpress.com

Design by Bashan Aquart
Printed in China

1 2 3 4 5 6 7 8 9 0
First Edition

The GOOD HUSBAND GUIDE

GUIDE

19 Tips
for
Domestic Bliss

A PRINCE AMONG MEN

IF A MAN'S HOME IS HIS CASTLE, well then, doesn't that make you a princess? A top-drawer fellow will make his wife feel like queen for a day, every day, with thoughtful gestures like serving her breakfast in bed, drawing her bubble bath in the evening, offering up a daily foot rub, and never forgetting to tell her that he would be a mere shell of a man without her.

Isn't He Dreamy?

WITH THE HANDSOME URBANITY of Cary Grant, the rugged swagger of John Wayne, and the boyish charm of Troy Donahue, your husband will be deemed "the bee's knees" by the ladies in your coffee klatch when he confidently comports himself like a gentleman from the silver screen. Yet rest assured, his iron-clad fidelity and unwavering adoration for you mean you'll never have to share the title of "leading lady" in his heart.

KNIGHT *in*
SHINING ARMOR

AN IDEAL HUSBAND will shield his lady love from all that is unseemly or indelicate in this world. Such duties include the disposal of household rubbish, cleaning up after the family pet, and the extermination of errant insects. When circumstances dictate, the man of the house will also spare his wife the burden of incorrigible children, meddling in-laws, and tedious dinners with colleagues.

No Fuss, No Muss!

A TITAN OF TIDINESS, your considerate spouse takes special care not to leave detritus in his wake. Not only will he place his clothes in the laundry hamper and deposit his dirty dishes in the sink, he'll also take the initiative to straighten up the house whenever and wherever he spies an item out of place. Only be forewarned: ever preoccupied with household gadgets and machinery, you'll be hard pressed to tear him away from that vacuum cleaner!

Rule #5

Dapper Dan

AN UPWARDLY MOBILE MAN dresses for success. Sure, those dungarees may fit him in all the right places when he's doing yard work or toiling under the hood of his Corvette, but he'll cut a truly dashing figure in a bespoke suit, crisp seersucker slacks, or spiffy pair of khakis. And since a man with this level of sartorial sense needs an equally well-dressed mate, he'll never look at you askance when you splurge at the local dressmaker's shop or buy your third handbag this week.

What a Knockout!

BULGING BICEPS aren't just window dressing. A merit-worthy mister puts his brawn to good use by opening tight jar-lids, changing flat tires, shoveling the drive, and engaging in any household chore predicated on the use of sheer force and elbow grease. Certainly your fragile constitution and dainty frame couldn't be expected to take on such grunt work as scrubbing the kitchen floor or defrosting the Frigidaire!

RULE #7 # Cool Daddy-O

FOREVER INDEBTED TO YOU for delivering his progeny to the world, your grateful mate should feel inspired to do his part as the family patriarch. When diaper-duty or 2 a.m. feedings are on the agenda, he'll answer the call with aplomb. You can count on him to clean pureed peas off your two-year-old or placate your tantrum-throwing pre-teen. Sigh no more, exhausted mothers — truly, this father knows best.

Mr. Fix-It

STEP ASIDE, NASA, and meet a tech-savvy marvel able to fix anything that goes on the fritz using little more than duct tape and an Allen wrench. We all know how much he enjoys tinkering with his tool-set and tackling those "Honey Do" lists you present him with each Saturday morning. Feeling useful is every man's greatest aim in life, so don't deprive him of his chance to prove himself handy.

Palling Around

ALTHOUGH HE'D NATURALLY RATHER BE home with you chatting about feelings or helping fold laundry, occasionally, "Boys' Night" will beckon. Don't begrudge your spouse's Elk Club membership or nickel poker games. It's harmless fun, and he's sure to be home by nine. Better yet, all that male bonding will have him pining for a little female companionship, if you sense our meaning!

"TACT"-ICAL MANEUVERS

A GOOD HUSBAND UNDERSTANDS that there is a right and wrong way for broaching certain subject matter. Like a U.N. diplomat on the eve of a cold-war showdown, he'll parse his words delicately when weighing in on your daring new bouffant haircut or your experimental parsnip-and-liverwurst casserole. To that end, he always manages to gift-wrap his gentle criticisms with a ribbon of good cheer.

Lip Service

MODERN MAN HAS CERTAINLY evolved from the days of caveman grunts and monosyllabic responses. Today, courtesy and compliments are at the heart of pleasing marital discourse. From proclamations of praise to whispered sweet nothings, you'll blush and bask in his daily declarations of admiration. A worthy gent also listens as skillfully as he speaks, clicking off the television or putting away the newspaper to give you his undivided attention.

Self-Sacrifice

WHEN YOU NOBLY URGE YOUR husband to partake of the last slice of apple brown betty, he honorably insists, "Oh, no, my pet! *You* deserve the last piece!" Ever putting your needs and wants ahead of his own, he will do things like brave below-zero temperatures to scrape the ice off your car's windshield, hold your purse while you scrutinize a sale rack, or leave his sick bed to climb on the roof and fix the TV antenna.

Groomed to Perfection

HOW IS IT THAT HE MANAGES TO LOOK — and smell — so deliciously manly? Chalk it up to the extra effort he makes in the realm of personal grooming. With some minor snipping and trimming, a handful of pomade, and a spritz of cologne, he'll leave you wistful for those teenage excursions up to Promontory Point. Speaking of yesteryear, did we mention that his waist size hasn't changed since the day you two lovebirds met? He'll leave the pot bellies to the pigs and the stoves, thank you very much!

He Shouldn't Have!

REMINDING HIM ABOUT YOUR upcoming anniversary is about as necessary as reminding the sun to rise. While his acknowledgment of the special days in your life is to be expected, the great lengths he'll go to in honor of those celebrations will leave you, quite simply, breathless. Brace yourself for surprise jaunts to Paris, bottles of chilled Dom Perignon in front of a crackling fire, and more diamonds than could be found in Liz Taylor's safe-deposit box!

Your Daily
Pick-Me-Up

SOME DAYS ARE TRAGIC. When you ruin a freshly polished manicure, scrape the fender on the Packard, or accidentally deflate the soufflé intended for tonight's dinner, it's natural to find yourself in a sour mood. Luckily, your understanding husband will be your antidote (key word: *dote*). You'll be purring like a kitten by the time he's finished pampering and waiting on you hand and foot.

Spicing Things Up

THE ONLY MONOTONY IN YOUR relationship will be the weekly delivery of fresh-cut flowers from your dear Don Juan. Otherwise, he'll keep you on your toes with spontaneous gestures of romance that will reignite those initial sparks of attraction. By day he may by your beast of burden, but when the sun sets, hes a tiger in the bedroom!

ONE OF THE GIRLS

A GOOD HUSBAND always takes an interest in his wife's favorite hobbies and pursuits, and he'll gladly join in on those activities. So go ahead — invite him to go caroling in Victorian garb, include him in your book club meetings, or sign him up for ballroom dance lessons. Even if an event coincides with the big game he's been gearing up for, he'll happily trade in his tickets to revel in the splendor of your favorite pastime.

Man OF Means

HE DOESN'T JUST BRING HOME THE BACON — he brings home the whole hog, and that's how he prefers to spend it, too. Sure, he'll invest wisely so as to save up for that sailboat and second home you've always dreamed about. But in the meantime, he's happy to treat his doll to the finer things in life. No more clipping coupons — your Mr. Wonderful isn't afraid to spread the wealth.

A BORN LEADER

WITH HIS WIT, wisdom, and humble regard for humanity, your husband prompts the awe and respect of strangers, who whisper amongst themselves, "Is he a Kennedy?" Sure, he seems born for high political office, but who needs the drama? He asks not what he can do for his country — only what he can do for you, his darling wife!

ABOUT LADIES' HOMEMAKER MONTHLY

LADIES' HOMEMAKER MONTHLY was a preeminent homemaker's journal at the turn of the last century. Located in the Midwest, its editors strongly advocated the temperance movement and old-fashioned family values. Their most famous adage was "You can judge a good woman by how many well-dressed children she has and the contentment of her husband."

ABOUT CIDER MILL PRESS BOOK PUBLISHERS

GOOD IDEAS RIPEN WITH TIME. From seed to harvest, Cider Mill Press strives to bring fine reading, information, and entertainment together between the covers of its creatively crafted books. Our Cider Mill bears fruit twice a year, publishing a new crop of titles each spring and fall.

Visit us on the web at
www.cidermillpress.com

or write to us at
12 Port Farm Road
Kennebunkport, Maine